ANIMAL CHAMPIONS OF THE MOUNTAINS

By Mignonne Gunasekara

BookLife
PUBLISHING

BookLife Publishing Ltd.
King's Lynn
Norfolk, PE30 4LS

Printed in Malta.

A catalogue record for this book is available from the British Library.

ISBN: 978-1-83927-452-7

Written by:
Mignonne Gunasekara

Edited by:
Emilie Dufresne

Designed by:
Drue Rintoul

Photo Credits

All images are courtesy of Shutterstock.com. With thanks to Getty Images, Thinkstock Photo and iStockphoto. Throughout – totally out. Front Cover – notsuperstar, Ramon Carretero, Eric Isselee. 2–3 – soft_light. 4–5 – Lisa Stelzel, Robert Frashure. 6–7 – Daniel Prudek. 8–9 – chbaum, Chris Desborough, Eric Isselee. 10–11 – pickypalla, Pavel Svoboda Photography, Tina Andros. 12–13 – S.R. Maglione, moosehenderson. 14–15 – Ondrej Prosicky, RealityImages, Hugh Lansdown. 16–17 – Michael Roeder, Ondrej Prosicky. 18–19 – ArCaLu, Giedriius, Daria Rybakova. 20–21 – Olga Savina, Art_mriia. 22–23 – Amelia Fox, NYS, Sakura Image Inc, Monkey Business Images.

CONTENTS

Words that look like this can be found in the glossary on page 24.

UP THE MOUNTAIN

Living on a mountain can be difficult – it may be hard to find food, it may be cold, and it may even be hard to find a safe place to step...

Let's meet the animal champions that call the mountains their home!

WHAT MAKES AN ANIMAL CHAMPION?

Animal champions don't always have to be the biggest, fastest, or strongest animals around. They are special because of the adaptations they have, or things they can do.

Come on! Let's head up the mountain...

WILD YAK

Wild yaks can live at heights of around 6,000 metres. It is very cold this high up – the temperature can get as low as -40 degrees Celsius.

Champion of Staying Warm

Yaks have thick fur coats that keep them warm.

The air is thin at this height. This can make it hard to breathe, but yaks have an adaptation to help them. They have big lungs.

Champion of Breathing Big

A yak's lungs can hold three times the air a cow's lungs can.

SNOW LEOPARD

The colours and patterns of a snow leopard's thick fur coat allow it to blend into its rocky, mountain surroundings, making it harder to spot. This is called camouflage.

Champion of Camouflage

A snow leopard's fluffy fur coat keeps it warm.

A snow leopard has a long tail that helps it balance as it climbs. It also has long, powerful back legs that help it leap really far.

Snow leopards sometimes use their long tails as a blanket.

ALPACA

Alpacas can live at heights of up to 4,800 metres. Not many plants grow at these heights, so alpacas must be careful not to damage the grasses and shrubs they eat.

Alpacas live in herds.
This helps to keep them safe.

An alpaca's feet are soft and padded so they step lightly. This means they can graze without damaging the plants around them.

MOUNTAIN LION

Mountain lions are also known as cougars or pumas. They are fast runners and can change direction quickly while running because of their bendy spines.

Champion of Speed

Mountain lions often stalk animals before jumping out and killing them.

If a mountain lion cannot finish its food in one go, it will hide the food under leaves and come back to eat it later.

Mountain lions are good jumpers because of their strong legs.

KIANG

Kiang can live at heights of over 4,000 metres, where they mostly eat grasses. When there is plenty of food around, kiang can put on up to 45 kilograms in body weight.

Champion of Sticking Together

There can be up to 400 kiang in one herd!

A kiang's coat changes throughout the year. In winter, it is longer, thicker and brown in colour. In summer, it is shorter, thinner and more reddish in colour.

Champion of Changing with the Seasons

EURASIAN LYNX

The Eurasian lynx lives in snowy forests. It has long legs to keep its body off the snow, and its coat grows thicker in winter to keep it extra warm.

Champion of Living in the Snow

Big, furry paws help the Eurasian lynx walk on snow.

Eurasian lynxes are very stealthy. This means they are often not seen or heard. They don't usually make sounds and they love to hide behind bushes and plants.

BROWN BEAR

Brown bears eat a lot of food in the autumn, which makes them put on a lot of fat. The fat stored in their bodies is used to keep them going through their long winter hibernation.

Brown bears are strong and good at digging. They dig into the mountainside to make their dens. Dens are safe spaces for them to sleep in.

They also dig into the ground to find animals to eat.

NUBIAN IBEX

The Nubian ibex is an amazing climber. It can even climb up the sides of cliffs! This helps it move around the rocky mountains it calls home while staying one step ahead of predators.

Champion of Climbing

The sun can be very strong up in the mountains. The Nubian ibex has a shiny coat that the sunlight bounces off, keeping the ibex cool.

Champion of Staying Cool

BECOMING A CHAMPION

Let's see what animal adaptations we humans can use to be champions of the mountain!

A warm coat does the same job as a yak's thick fur.

Snowshoes or boots will help you walk in the snow like a lynx.

Camouflage will help you hide like a snow leopard.

A spade will help you dig like a bear.

GLOSSARY

adaptations	changes that have happened to an animal over time and help them to be better suited to their environment
balance	the ability to stay upright
direction	the way that someone or something is moving
graze	eat grass in a field
herds	large groups of animals that live together
hibernation	spending the winter in a very deep sleep
predators	animals that hunt other animals for food
shrubs	low-growing plants that usually have lots of stems
spines	backbones
stalk	to follow someone or something without being noticed

INDEX